# Love Poems: Are You The One?

By: Steve Ryan

©Copyright 2013 by Steve Ryan
Love Poems: Are You The One?
ISBN-13: 978-0615937946 (Steve Ryan)
ISBN-10: 0615937942
Published by: Steve Ryan Publishing

# Table of Contents

Introduction..................................................5
**Chapter 1 Dreaming of Love........................ 6**
Where Are You My One?............................. 7
Imagining Love........................................... 8
I'm Sorry for the Mixed Signals................... 9
My Love Dream..........................................10
What is the Problem?.................................11
Tired of Dreaming About Love....................12
Our Unexpected Meet.................................13
Can We Save What We Had?......................14
Should I Hope for Love?.............................15
I Met You in My Sleep................................16
**Chapter 2 Falling in Love.......................... 17**
We Can Make This Last............................. 18
A True Romance....................................... 19
The Sweet Aroma......................................20
A Love Holiday..........................................21
We Met By Design..................................... 22
When We First Met....................................23
You're the Only One.................................. 24
It's the Same When Time Goes By..................25
This Love is Taking Over Me......................26
**Chapter 3 The Relationship...................... 27**
Should I Buy My Lady A Diamond Ring?..........28
Come Over Here and Talk to Me................... 29
Our Love Harmony.................................... 30
What Are You Thinking?........................... 31
Do I Need to Worry?................................. 32
All About You........................................... 33
Will You Commit or Surrender Me?.............. 34
Love Me for Life or Let Me Go.................... 35
I Love Our Moments................................. 36
You're Taking Me for Granted..................... 37

# Table of Contents

**Chapter 4 Heartbreak............................. 38**
Screw This, I'm Done................................. 39
My Heart Bleeds....................................... 40
Your Cheating Ways..................................41
Why Do You Hurt Me?.............................. 42
It's Time for Me to Leave............................ 43
The Anger Inside of You............................ 44
Love's History.......................................... 45
You Revealed the Truth.............................. 46
Beginning to Fall...................................... 47
I'm Willing to Change................................ 48
**Chapter 5 Reconnect or Move on................. 49**
Walk in the Park.......................................50
Goodbye My Past Love, Goodbye...................51
Is it a Mistake?........................................ 52
I Miss You.............................................. 53
I'm Over The Anger.................................. 54
I Must Move On....................................... 55
Don't Tell Me.......................................... 56
I'm Still in Love With You........................... 57
This In-between Game................................58
Reconnecting to Your Energy........................59

## Introduction

"Love Poems: Are You The One?" digs deep into the heart of love. These poems and insights are written in a way that most people will relate to. There are many questions that people ask about love. Here are some of those questions. When am I going to find "The One"? Is the person that I'm with "The One"? Are we going to work out? How does this person feel about me? What does this person think about me? This book addresses many love situations. It will answer some of the questions that people want answered.

Most people have gone through some type of experience involving love. Some people get lucky and find the right person for them and they spend the rest of their lives with that person. Other people are not so lucky and they go through different experiences from falling in love to heartbreak. And after the heartbreak, the famous questions arise, "Will We Reconnect?" or "Should I Just Move on?. "Love Poems: Are You The One?" addresses those different experiences and cycles that people go through.

This book is divided into five chapters; Dreaming of Love, Falling in Love, The Relationship, Heartbreak and Reconnect or Move on. Each chapter has a word of insight about the topic at the beginning of the chapter. Following the insight will be a collection of poems about the topic of the chapter. You will find the poems very enjoyable but insightful at the same time. Enjoy the experience and begin your journey through "Love Poems: Are You The One?".

# Chapter 1 - Dreaming of Love

The Dreaming of Love stage is a territory that is often visited. This is where people fantasize about who is the one for them. For some people who are not in relationships, they question when they will find the one. For others who are in unfulfilled or unsatisfying relationships, they ask themselves if their partner is the one and if not, they wonder when they will find the one.

What is the one? People have different meanings for this. Is it the man or woman of your dreams? Is it just a physical connection? Is it more than physical? Does it involve a deeper connection such as a deep emotional or spiritual connection? After coming across so many people and seeing different experiences, I've come to the conclusion that "the one" will vary from person to person.

People evolve and grow. Have you ever found yourself not attracted to things that you once were attracted to? What about the opposite, are you now attracted to things that you weren't attracted to in the past? Maybe you want someone taller or shorter. Or perhaps, you're attracted to a different personality. Maybe you want someone who is more outgoing or someone who is more introverted.

One common thing that I've seen in some people may or may not shock you. They are attracted to someone that gives them a challenge. I'm sure this isn't the case for every single person, but let's face it; it is human nature for some people to want what they think they can't have. At last we begin Dreaming of Love.

## Where are you my one?

I can see you
Your image is in my head
We met in my dreams
Although we've never met

I can envision your beauty
In many ways it turns me on
I feel this so strong
This feeling can't be wrong

I can picture us together side by side
You're everything to me, my heart is open wide
I can see us talking about so many things
I can see us picking out our wedding rings

You're the one for me and I am for you
The spark we feel gives away the clues
When I'm around you, I can't help but smile
You complete me; I want us to have a child

The love that we feel it is so rare
The passion that we feel makes our eyes glare
When we finally meet, this will be our truth
Where are you my one, where do I find you?

# Imagining Love

I try to imagine real love
What is it like? How will it come?
Will I feel butterflies?
Or is that a myth and a lie?

What if love sneaks up on me?
Before I know it, I'll have a family
Will it catch me by total surprise?
Am I ready to be satisfied?

What if love comes in a different way?
If it comes overnight, what will I say?
I'm imagining this day in my dreams
Until I see it, finding real love is a mystery

I don't know how this will happen
I'll try each day to take some action
If I focus on making me a better me
Then attracting true love will be a reality

Until that happens I have imagination
I can picture true love through many stages
I can see us spending time on the beach
We'll hold hands until the sun retreats

I'll hold you in my arms as the moonlight shine down
I'll be your heat when the cool breeze comes around
We'll be happy as we're having all this fun
We'll fall asleep together until the morning sun

This is how I imagine a day with my true love
Come to me now; embrace me with your hug
I know that this time is coming near
Maybe true love will happen this year

## I'm Sorry for the Mixed Signals

We met each other recently
It was a nice meet
What am I supposed to feel?
How do I know if this is true love?

We bonded so nice
You were very attractive
I can't find anything wrong
Is this too good to be true?

I could see myself falling in love with you
But I'm an idiot, I backed off from you
I went cold and I went silent
I let fear take over and didn't know what to do

I know you're probably wondering what went wrong
You didn't do anything to deserve this sad song
Maybe I was too caught up in my own dream
You were finally here and all I did was freeze

I had this idea of what my true love would be
You were very close to that reality
To be honest, it scared me
I'm in so much shock, I just can't believe

What should I do?
What should I say?
I can't expect you to understand
Or to give me a break

I'm sorry for the mixed signals
I was wrong
I didn't mean to hurt you
I'm just used to being alone

## My Love Dream

I dream and imagine
That I'll find "The One" someday
When I find you,
What will I say?

I'm looking for the full package
Can I want what I give?
Is it wrong to want beauty inside and out?
I want to enjoy my soul mate as we live

Will you be easy to talk to?
Can I let my guards down?
My heart is what you'll see through
I have nothing to hide

Will I have to sacrifice what I want?
No one's perfect, we all have faults
Will you hold my attention?
Or will I be lost in my own thoughts?

These are some questions that enter my mind
As I think about my future valentine
I look forward to seeing the unseen
As I explore My Love Dream

## What is the Problem?

Love, why haven't you happened already?
Did I do something wrong?
Why do you keep sending losers my way?
Is this karma correcting the day?

Am I being punished for my past?
I didn't mean to pass up a past chance
I wasn't ready for love then
I needed to grow for a true commitment

Now that I'm ready
No one catches my eye
I don't feel any sparks
Even when there's an attractive outside

I need a certain feeling
One that's deeper and more
I'm not going to sacrifice and settle
I don't want to be bored

I'm trying to be patient, but this is getting hard
Something's got to give, I need a new start
Sometimes I feel like giving up on this dream
Is true love really meant for me?

## Tired of Dreaming about Love

Sometimes I get tired of dreaming about love
Maybe I need a break from it
It's become a habit
Now it's not fun

Is love overrated?
Does happiness really exist?
Can true love really happen?
Or is this just an unreal wish?

My thoughts have become stressful
Thinking about the romantic possibilities
Am I being too restless?
I want love to happen naturally

It's hard to escape the mention of love
It's shown everywhere around
It's on the TV, the radio and the movies
You can't escape love's town

I wonder if the desire is created
From all the things that we see
Is love seriously for real?
Or is it just a dream?

I hope the answer comes
I don't want to be without
It would be nice to experience
This love that everyone talks about

## Our Unexpected Meet

When I first met you
We shared a kiss
It was unexpected
Wow, oh the magic

Then you went away
I thought I had your number saved
Somehow I lost it
I wish your flight was delayed

Now I can't find you
I don't know your last name
I'm feeling so frustrated
This is love lost, I'm ashamed

It was something about you
You're all in my head
I don't know what to do
Will we run into each other again?

I wish you had my number
But your phone wasn't charged
I can't believe I saved yours wrong
Now I'm singing sad love songs

This love is so lost
Now it's only in my dreams
I knew that you were the one
Will you be in my future?
Life, please answer that mystery.

## Can We Save What We Had?

Am I wrong to be in love with another?
Although I'm committed to you
I don't know why this is happening
What should I do?

I'm trying hard to make us work
But it's not right to deceive my heart
I don't think I'm in love with you anymore
You're taking me for granted and I need more

Staying in love can't be a routine
We must keep it interesting and change the scene
Love is like a flower that needs water to grow
To deny this will make our sparkle not show

You've changed how you treated me over time
We don't talk anymore, now I feel we're in a lie
You just assume that I will always be there
Now I feel imprisoned and it's not fair

This opened the door for my heart to be open
And now I'm having dreams about love with another
Don't get me wrong, I will never cheat
I'm a faithful person and I believe in honesty

Something has to change or we're going to end
We have to rebuild our relationship and start again
I hope that you're open to a brand new start
If you're not, then you're going to lose me in my heart

I don't want to hurt you or hurt me
We have to get sincere and rekindle our dream
I want us to last and I want it to be life long
Please help us and be open to correcting this wrong

## Should I Hope for Love?

Does real love exist?
Or is it just a figment of our imagination?
These are questions that come in my mind
I've been in and out of love through time

How does love survive and weather the storm?
Was this the way we're designed when we're born?
I'm trying to figure this out so I won't forget
What is this true love so that I know what to expect?

Why is it that we can be in love one minute?
And then the next, we fall out of love?
What does this really mean?
Was our love true from the beginning?

I question these things from experience
It's been more than once that I was in it
When I thought that I had found the one
In a blink of an eye, we were done

This quest for love is like a huge mystery
I'm running out of patience and energy
I don't know if I can go through it one more time
Falling in and out of love is tearing my mind

What is the meaning of all of this?
Is life and love just a big game?
I admit sometimes it is fun
But this up and down is getting lame

I guess I will move forward down this road
It can't hurt to have a glimmer of hope
Love, if you're out there and you really exist
I need you to step forward out of this nothingness

## I Met You in My Sleep

I woke up from a deep sleep last night
And I thought about what I'd seen
I saw your face as I was holding you tight
You were the star in my dreams

I feel the warmness that's here with us
As I hold you in my arms
I'm the luckiest person in the world
You broke me with your charm

You're the only person that's for me
You're my princess, you're my queen
There's no one else like you in this world
You're number one, there are no other girls

This is the way that I feel
Look inside me and hear my truth
Our love is deep and real
For you, any mountain I would move

I believe this was a vision
Of how our love will be
I'm looking forward to that future
Too bad this was just a dream

I can't wait to meet you in person
When our souls find each other
The wait will be worth it
Our connection will be discovered

# Chapter 2 - Falling In Love

Falling in love is an awesome feeling. I've been there before. There's a lot of excitement when you are first falling in love. A lot of people want it and crave it. Just imagine how many love songs, love movies and other topics of love that's out there. It's one of the most talked about topics. The feeling of knowing that you can have a potential life mate to create a life with can seem very fulfilling.

There were several questions that I've had when I fell in love in the past. Is what I'm feeling real? Is this truly falling in love, or is this just the rush and excitement from meeting someone new where there is mutual attraction? Then the little birdy whispers in my ear and says, is this going to be something that works or will I get hurt?

Different people react to the fear of falling in love in different ways. Some people ignore it and go full steam ahead. Others come across as giving mixed signals because their heart is fighting their head. The heart is saying, give this a shot. But the head is saying, run, run, run.

I don't believe in letting fear rule the heart. At the same time, I do believe that learning from past experiences can help us make stronger decisions in the future. If you're experiencing falling in love at this moment, my advice to you is to enjoy it. Take it one moment and one day at a time. Pay attention to the signs and clues over time.

If your mind, your gut feeling and the practical elements are in alignment with your heart, then it's most likely a good situation for you. On the other hand, if something doesn't feel right, then just make sure that you pay attention to any red flags. This will help to decide if you need to continue or exit the situation. These are some thoughts on Falling in Love.

## We Can Make This Last

We've been spending a lot of time together
Since the first day we met
The connection between us is like stormy weather
It stirs up all the love thoughts in our heads

I feel like we're falling for each other
There's no denying it
The way we act when we're together
It makes it so obvious

Anytime that we're apart
I can't get you out of my head
Are you going through the same thing?
I was in doubt but you confirmed it instead

It feels so good to be in sync
Our love has just begun
I've waited so long for this moment
When I can say I'm falling in love

We're moving at a nice pace
Things aren't going too fast
We're taking the solid way
This is how relationships last

## A True Romance

When we stare into each other's eyes
The chemistry is no surprise
We feel each other's thoughts
Our emotions are so high

We're stuck in a daze
All our past baggage fades away
It doesn't matter what didn't work before
We're connected so deep, it opens love's door

We can sit and talk all day
With you everything is easy to say
I don't have to wonder what's on your mind
Your words flow so well, and it makes time fly by

I enjoy being around you
Every time we meet, there's something new
You always look so well
I can feel my heart move

You know that we're falling in love
I can feel it when we're holding hands
When we touch, we go into a trance
This is real, we have a true romance

## The Sweet Aroma

How sweet is that aroma?
It smells like roses that are one of a kind
The air is filled with our love and it's taking over
You are the only thing that's on my mind

When your presence meets mine
Paradise begins
I then begin to hope
That our paradise never ends

You define true beauty
It shows inside and out
Everything with you is so natural
I need you and can't go without

How sweet is that aroma?
It smells like fresh air
Our love isn't just one moment
We have the rest of our lives to share

This is our new start
The beginning of falling in love
We have what it takes to make this work
Our fire will stay lit and shine above

## A Love Holiday

You have me singing all day long
I'm listening to nothing but love songs
Today is the day that my walls fell
I have drank water from love's well

What have you done to me?
I can't eat and I can't sleep
I want you close, I want you near
Let's be together and bring in a new year

You were the first to say you're in love
I couldn't speak, the cat had my tongue
When I couldn't respond, I felt so bad
Did I push you away or make you mad?

I was finally able to speak
I'm glad that you listened
I'm strong but your love made me weak
When I said this, we started kissing

I'm glad that we are sharing our love
We've made an explosion
There is nothing that's standing in our way
We have declared today a love holiday

## We Met By Design

Can you believe we're already planning our wedding?
We just met three months ago, where are we heading?
I'm caught up in the excitement of all this love
But it feels so real, experiencing this was my first

I always took longer in my past
I've never gotten into a relationship this fast
You felt so right and this couldn't be wrong
We knew each other all long

We knew each other before we met
It was like a decade in the first second
I smiled ear to ear with a big grin
As soon as we met, I knew this was a win

We talked about our future on that first day
And to our surprise, we wanted the same thing
We were in sync, we were already one
Our spirits were married in the soul sun

It was by design that we met
Our connection was confirmed in an instant
And now today we are making progress
I welcome our future, there are no regrets

## When We First Met

When we first met
It was like magic
We fit so well together
We had a natural attraction

When I looked into your eyes
You reached out for my hand
That first kiss was a surprise
It ignited a new romance

When we first held each other
I didn't want to let go
That moment was real and special
It wasn't just a show

Anytime that we're together
We make each other smile
That stays in my mind forever
I get excited like a child

When I hear your voice
I start to melt inside
It's so smooth and sweet
It keeps me mesmerized

When I kiss your sexy lips
Mmmm is all I can say
We had this natural connection
Ever since that first day

## You're the Only One

You're the only one
That I'm thinking of
We've fallen in love
You're like the stars shining above

From the very first moment
That I saw your face
I knew that moment was it
Everything fell into place

When we first kissed
Everything was confirmed
This was no accident
We were comfortable with no concerns

As time moved on
Our connection stayed strong
You mean the world to me
I've seen how much we've grown

We keep each other centered
We have honesty
No bad thing will enter
You're the only one for me

## It's the Same When Time Goes By

Why do I like you so much?
What is it that you do?
Is it the magic from your touch?
Or is it the emotions from being with you?

When I first met you
This was not something that I'd foreseen
This feeling crept up on me
Before I could blink, we created history

Everything is a blur
Right now and back then
A year flew by like a second
But our love feelings still stand

Our love is still the same
The strength of it hasn't changed
Wow, this has left me amazed
It's like every day is our honeymoon phase

The energy between us is always like the first time
Is this normal to constantly blow my mind?
When we're together we do a lot of kissing
We enjoy life and we're ready for our commitment

## This Love is Taking Over Me

I've been sitting here all alone
Just thinking about you coming home
It's only been a few hours since we've touched
But baby my heart is missing you so much

It's hard to concentrate with my time
I can't get you off my mind
I'm thinking about what you said when you were leaving
You admitted being in love and there was no questioning

It shocked me because I was thinking the same thing
I'm ready for you to move in; I want to give you a ring
Although you have your home and I have mine
You're always over here all the time

We're like a married couple with the way that we act
I always look forward to you coming back
Your clothes are here and it's like you've moved in
You'll be back tonight and I can't wait until then

This love is taking over me
Is this real or is this a dream?
Our emotions come so intensely
I want you right here, next to me

When we're together I feel so free
But when we're apart it's hard to sleep
The feelings are mutual I do understand
I'm going to do my best to be a good man

# Chapter 3 – The Relationship

If you are in a relationship, how does it feel to you? It can take a lot of work to get into a successful relationship. Relationships have their different stages. You meet, get to know one another, date and eventually you get into the relationship. The speed and the requirements that people have on each other will vary situation to situation.

There are a few things that comes to people's mind when they think about a relationship. Can I trust this person? Is this going to work out? Is this person being faithful? Does this have long term potential? There isn't a way to know these things every step along the way. Relationships have so many dynamics to them. Some of those dynamics are compatibility with each other, personalities, level of connection and a trust factor.

In my opinion, I feel that relationships work out best when people can accept their partner as they are. One of the biggest things that I've seen in relationships that don't work is when one person tries to force change on the other person. This leads to feelings of being taken for granted, being controlled and an imbalance in the relationship. Either two people fit for each other or they don't. Don't get me wrong, change can be good. Especially when there are damaging habits. However, when it starts to become a situation to where you're trying to force someone to change, that can be a problem.

The key to a relationship working out is good communication, learning to understand your partner and accepting the fact that no situation is going to be perfect. And if those things are in place and your partner isn't being a negative impact on your life, then the relationship have a lot of potential to work out. We now introduce, the Relationship.

## Should I Buy My Lady A Diamond Ring?

I'm just sitting here on this endless delay
Allowing my time to flow away
I'm thinking about that April spring
Should I buy my lady a diamond ring?
There is nothing here that's in this world
That is better than my special girl
So it's time to let my true love sing
Should I buy my lady that diamond ring?

She's been there for me through thick and thin
And her patience with me, it never caves in
It's time to show my appreciation
By giving her my full dedication
I will keep our flame forever lit and from dying
Whatever it takes, I will keep on trying
This isn't some line that is used for lying
Her unconditional love for me, is so inspiring

It feels so good to make her feel wanted
She deserves the best, she deserves to flaunt it
I've decided to make a go at this theme
It's time to buy my lady a diamond ring.
Can a flame stay burning without feeding it?
Can a flower stay growing without being grounded?
So I can't expect my lady to be any different
I must nurture her and care and show her I mean it

Besides, what is this thing called money
It can't feed you like milk and honey
For it cannot be compared to love
And you can't take it with you to the sky above
So instead of holding on to it in a cheap way
Why not use it to show I want my lady to stay
This is why I'm doing the right thing
By buying my lady that diamond ring

## Come Over Here and Talk to Me

Come over here and talk to me
I can tell what you're thinking
Don't let the anger continue to be
I don't want our relationship sinking
You are playing hard to get
Why can't you let it go?
I don't like arguing
When will our love reappear and show?

So come over here and talk with me
Let me hold your hand
I don't know even know what you're mad about
I want to understand
We were fine just a moment ago
And then your demeanor changed
Now the frown on your face shows
And you're rolling your eyes this way

Please come over here and talk to me
I want to fix what is wrong
Do we have a real problem?
Or is this your way to get attention all along?
I think that's what this is
You love to make up
Now I'm starting to solve this
You're just making a fake fuss

You finally decided to talk to me
And you told me what was wrong
You were upset over the smallest thing
And you just wanted a hug
I think that you find this fun
You like to stir a little drama between us
Does this make you feel loved?
Don't worry, we're solid and we have a lot of trust

## Our Love Harmony

I love it when we're in harmony
When we're in tune our love sings
Although sometimes we're on different notes
We are always on the same page

When our love is playing a major key
That's when our thoughts are in sync
We see the big picture that shows where we're heading
Our timing is on and we have understanding

But then there are times where our tuning is off
Those are the times where we seem lost
These moments catch us off guard and give us surprise
We have to slow the tempo when those conflicts arise

It doesn't mean that we have to start over
We can keep playing until our tunes meet
This is how we get back on the same beat
Solving our problems makes us strong and not weak

Sometimes our love plays a minor key
That's when minor details are made reality
It's hard to plan those moments, let's play it by ear
We're two different people, but that won't interfere

Overall I like us singing our love song
Our relationship is solid and it survives our wrong
And even when there are times that we disagree
Our love will survive, this is what I see

## What Are You Thinking?

What do you think about me?
Do you enjoy our company?
I want to know what you're thinking
What are your plans and your intentions?

Can you see us lasting for the long term?
Or am I just an in the moment crush?
I need a sign and need some validation
I need to know that my time isn't wasting

I do enjoy the moment
I enjoy what we have
But sometimes we're in limbo
And confusion deals its hand

I don't want to do anything
That will drive you away
But I need some confirmation
Or I'll be the one to not stay

I've been through a lot of hurt
I have to protect myself
I won't be treated like dirt
So step up and give me what I deserve

## Do I Need to Worry?

We've been together for a while
Your habits I have learned
I know your patterns and your style
Something's changed, should I be concerned?

Now you hide your phone
You go off to a corner to be alone
It's just a sneaky feeling
You're acting so suspicious

I'm not the type of person that's insecure
But you're being obvious with your shift
I don't believe in confusion
Your actions could end our relationship

I like to be straightforward and I am blunt
I asked you to tell me, is there something up?
In other words, it's time to be honest, what's going on?
Do I need to worry? Should I leave you alone?

I won't keep questioning this for long
I trust myself, my intuition isn't wrong
Things need to make sense some time real soon
I won't worry myself, I will just move

## All About You

Your smile is like the sun
That shines brightly over the sea
Your eyes are like the rain
It cast a spell on me

Your heart is like the moon
That lightens up the dark filled night
Your mind is like trees
It brings strength, power and might

Your dance is like the wind
It soothes me left and right
Your touch is like a magic hand
It brings relaxation inside

Your laugh is like the sunset
It's a warm summer breeze
Your talk is like an island
It has its own natural beauty

Being who you are is beautiful
That is the best way to stay
I think you are wonderful
You should never change

## Will You Commit or Surrender Me?

My love, I don't know what to say or do
I'm lost in a state in which I'm confused
I get so many signals that you're ready for commitment
But then reality brings me back to your contentment

And I see that you're happy with the way things are
You only want your heart to go so far
I have to protect me and my interest
I can't be in the game of pretending

I know there is a love that is mutual and it won't rest
But at the end of the day, my questions lead to stress
And I start to wonder how much I really mean to you
Would you even fight for me if my love was possible to lose?

Would you even cry for me if I decided to leave you?
I wonder what decision you would choose
My love, my heart is being torn apart
I can't remain in a love that has no path to start

I haven't exactly come to my decision
I want to react with proper precision
I don't want to let you go if real love has a chance
Some days I feel we have a true romance

I'm getting mixed signals that come straight from heart
Although your mouth says no to a long term relationship
Your actions says yes to a lifelong romantic start
So will you surrender me or will we have a true commitment?

Love Me For Life or Let Me Go

Is this just my imagination?
Am I driving myself to unwarranted tears?
You confused me with our conversation
Will we have regret in a few years?
I wish you would communicate
And tell me how you feel
Tell me what is going on
Tell me what is truly real

I feel love from you
When we kiss and when we touch
We can be around each other for hours
We never get tired no matter how much
I don't know what to do
Other than slowly back away from you
And if you truly want my heart
Then you'll fight for it before we grow apart

You won't let me walk out that door
Without crying that you want my love even more
And you already know my position
Our fate lies with your decision
I will leave our relationship in your hand
It will be your choice if you want long term romance
I feel what's in your heart
It's time to show me so that we have a real chance

So if you love me, please make a careful decision
I rather love you from a distance
Than to hate you when you're within inches
Love me for life or let me go

## I Love Our Moments

When I looked into your eyes
You make my heart beat faster
It races faster with every second in time
Our love that we feel is what matters

You made me feel some ways
Feelings I never felt before
I've had love in the past
But I've only been in love when you entered my door

I'm enjoying each moment
Every minute is great with you
My inside is filled with conflicted
My fear battles with truth

When we kiss, you feel so tender
You make my heart surrender
When we touch I feel the sensation
The intensity is so strong, how do I resist temptation?

A part of me feels that this happened so fast
But this connection was meant to last
From the first day, it was easy to talk to you
After we opened up, you didn't change your view

## You're taking me for granted

I feel that you're taking me for granted
If we keep doing this road
There won't be any love left standing
I'm not a robot that you can put on hold

Naturally I'm a nice person
That doesn't mean that I'm gullible
You can't put me on auto pilot
That is the start of our troubles

You have this impression
That you can treat me any way you wish
Love is a powerful emotion
But it needs to be fed to stay lit

It takes only a simple gesture
To show your appreciation
That will keep anger from festering
We can keep stable relations

Stop taking me for granted
Or I will be gone
This isn't an ultimatum
I just respect myself too much to be wronged

# Chapter 4 – Heartbreak

Heartbreak is one of the most painful emotions that can be felt. I would not wish heartbreak on anyone. It's hard enough to fall in love with the right person. When you add heartbreak into the mix, this creates fear, baggage and obstacles for any future love interests that you will have.

Have you ever been cheated on? Have you ever cheated? And if so, what made you do so? These are just a few of many things that can cause heartbreak. Heartbreak can cause hurt and feelings of lost after the end of a relationship.

It's hard to know when to end a relationship. Before I've ended previous relationships, I wondered several things. Is this the right thing to do? Am I rushing to judgment? Should I try to make this love work? Although those questions were thought about, the heartbreak at that time was inevitable.

I've seen other people deal with heartbreak in different ways. Some people jump right into something with a new person to help them get over the past person. Others take more time to heal and they need time before trusting again. Personally, when I've gone through heartbreak, I gave myself time to heal and I put closure to my past. I'm a naturally compassionate person, so I don't believe in bringing past baggage to a new relationship.

If you're dealing with heartbreak, don't suppress it. Allow yourself to deal with it so that you can move past it. With the right amount of time, heartbreak can heal. It doesn't mean that you have to stop loving the person. However, you can get to a point to where the heartbreak doesn't have to paralyze you and poison your heart with fear of being hurt again. This is the monster called Heartbreak.

## Screw this, I'm done

Will hatred be our future position?
I used to love you, but was my mind just kidding?
It's like I can't look at you anymore
Instead of love, hurt is what my heart stores

I gave my heart and my all to you
Time and time again you gave me bad news
I saw the signs but I didn't make an exit
Until you did the ultimate transgression

How can you do this to me right in my own bed?
You thought you were slick but I caught you instead
You had no idea that I was coming home
I was surprised that you weren't there alone

I am so hurt and it has turned into anger
Instead of being accountable, you're pointing your finger
How can this be on me? You're the one that's cheating
Screw this, I'm done, this time I'm leaving

## My Heart Bleeds

My heart bleeds
You know the reason why
You suddenly changed on me
And now my emotions make me cry
I was always there for you
There was only one thing that I ask
I wanted you to stay true
You couldn't do that, so we couldn't last

We traveled the world together
Anything we wanted was in our hands
We even talked of marriage
Now you've changed our circumstance
I can get over you in time
That won't be an my issue
It's the deception that is bothering me
All those times I kissed you

Were you pretending the whole time?
I thought what we had was real
I know I will bring in a better kind
Your actions broke our deal
We promised to always be there for each other
We vowed this while holding hands
I didn't do anything to deserve this
And now I've ended this romance

I will condition my heart
So that I can move on
In time I'll have the energy for a new start
It won't be with you, I want you gone
You can go anywhere you want
You just can't stay here
I'm not going to be weak in front of you
You will never see me shed a tear

## Your Cheating Ways

How dare you say I'm blind?
I know that you're a liar
You lie to me all the time
My rage builds up like fire

If you had to cheat
Then why didn't you just leave
Why hold on to me
Let's end this with some dignity

I knew something was going on
Your body language tells it all
You were acting different and distant
And then you made the wrong call

It's funny how the truth always comes out
There's no way to deny it
Your mistake revealed what was in the dark
And now there is no more trying

There is no excuse
To cause so much pain
I just wanted honesty
But all you've brought is shame

You broke up our happy home
Your deception did us wrong
I hope it was all worth it
No one's in your corner and you're alone

I gave you every opportunity
To end what we had
You begged me to stay with you
Why would you cheat after that?

## Why Do You Hurt Me?

Why do you treat me so bad?
I loved you as I loved myself
And you simply threw it all away
Why did you bother to greet me?

Why did you ever meet me?
I was there when there was no one there
To show support and undying love and loyalty
And my compensation was damnation

As I try to move on with my life
It is hard because you are constantly on my mind
And though I want to hate you
I now understand the thin line between love and hate

Although you've been horrible
I still care for you
It's just time to protect myself
I have to face the truth

You claim to want to be different
To be at peace and settle with one
But your ever cry is only words
No action is ever fulfilled from your tongue

## It's Time for Me to Leave

There is something that I want to confess
While you were thinking of me
I was not thinking about you
I just can't hurt you anymore
We've grown apart and so distant
I don't want you full of animosity
So the best thing that I can do
Is to just leave

You can have this house
I'll give you all the keys
I can't live here anymore
It's time for me to leave
Part of this is my fault
I knew this was coming
I should have opened up my mouth
And gave us a chance to solve it

You pushed me away
I just couldn't handle it
You neglected me for days
Those days became months and weeks
We're going through this routine
You know we're not happy
I don't think we can save this
This makes me feel so crappy

I thought we could work
I'm sorry I was wrong
We both should have what we deserve
Let's leave each other alone

The Anger Inside of You

I can feel your spirit
When I walked into the room
You have so much anger inside
What did I do to you?

Why are we not cool?
Is the hatred growing?
When you shut down on me
This is what you are implying

Things don't have to be this way
Talk to me, let's communicate
If you can't express to me what's wrong
Then we're working on our escape

Why did you ask me to stay?
If you had something wrong in your heart
If things keep going this way
We are destined to fall apart

It really makes me ache
We're at a breaking point
This is the sound of heartbreak
That sound makes so much noise

This anger is building inside of you
Everyone can tell
You won't give me any clues
And now our relationship will fail

Love's History

What becomes of a broken heart?
Will another love seem hard to start?
If you've been through love's game
Then your mind will understand what I say

I don't want to start again and again
Is this going to be my future history?
Heartbreak is no fun when you're in it
Is avoiding it a mystery?

I remember falling in love
How good it felt then
We put a lot of time into us
And then we headed for an end

I'm trying not to repeat
This same love history
I do truly believe
There's a solution for me

I'm going to be more patient
I'll trust my head and heart
The situation will have to be more stable
Before I let down my guard

This history has been painful
I'm working to overcome
I want balance, I know I'm able
To get past this and find my one

## You Revealed The Truth

You really hurt me last night
You made cry inside
I can't believe what I'm seeing
Someone else was kissing you
It's like my mind is deceiving
It's leaving me so confused

I won't put all the blame on you
I ignored what I felt, this isn't new
I saw the signs all around me
My gut had a message to see
But my heart wouldn't let me leave
And now it's torn apart from me

It's reality now that I see
There's no us
There's only you and then there's me
I thought we loved one another
That fantasy isn't true
Your lies was undercover
And now you revealed the truth

I must let you go
Although I love you so
Goodbye my love
Goodbye

## Beginning To Fall

We had just had a fight
Both of us were fuming and mad
We decided to talk
We expressed the feelings we had
We talked about how we felt
Then as we were siting in the car
We both were trying not to look at each other
Have we taken things too far?

And then something happened
We grabbed each other's hand
We both broke down
And expressed our romance
I told you how I felt
And you did the same
You told me I was a piece of you
And in your heart I'll always remain

I couldn't match the power
Of what you said with your words
But I felt the same as you did
I knew we were still in love
But our circumstances changed
And staying together created unrest
We needed to end based on logic
Separating was for the best

I didn't want to us end
We both still loved each other with our all
Why did life do this to us?
At that time, we were beginning to fall

## I'm willing to change

I can't believe it happened again
My will is gone, is this the end
My heart is broken I'm suffering
Things aren't the same since I lost my best friend

And I tell myself a thousand times
Someday I'll smile again
But until that day comes
I'll do my best with coping

I wish you didn't go
Why didn't I know?
I took our love for granted
You left so unexpected
I wish you didn't go

I need you in my life
I'm strong but now I'm crying
Believe in me
I'll be a better man
I'll change the way I am
And with you, I know I can

I'll sweep you off your feet
I'll show you how much you really mean to me
Our history won't repeat
My change is permanent
You'll see

# Chapter 5 – Reconnect or Move on

I've been through heartbreak before and I know some of you have too. One of the hardest decisions that some people have to make is what to do when someone you used to love resurfaces. If it was someone that you deeply cared about and was in love with at some point of time before, it's very hard to automatically keep that door shut. Of course, there are exceptions depending on how the relationship ended.

One of the questions that comes to mind is, "Do we reconnect or move on?" I've dealt with this situation before in my life. The first question that comes to mind is, why did the relationship end? Was it over a trust issue? Or was it the wrong timing? It's very nerve wrecking to wonder about the consequences of rekindling love with a past relationship. Will it be the same outcome that leads to the end of the relationship or will it actually workout?

When I was faced with this situation, I asked myself two things. Am I different now? Is my past love different as well? Did either one of us grow or make any changes? If we are the same people, what is going to make the situation work a second time around? Every situation is different.

In my opinion, I think that it's best to make sure that any decision you make isn't based on just emotions. The challenge is to make a decision based on balanced judgment. This means that you should do your best to not only take emotions into consideration, but also look at the practical elements around the situation as well.

One question that you should ask yourself is, "Am I a better person with or without this person in my life?" The answer to that question will help your decision as you decide if you should give your past love a try or if you should keep that door closed. What will the answer be? Should we "Reconnect or Move On?"

## Walk In the Park

I remember when we used to walk in the park
We used to look at the birds
We stayed until dark
There was a lot of sight seeing

We walked together side by side
Then we would sit on the bench
We would talk about the future
And how we would never split

Those were the days
When our love was strong and good
We were so in sync
Even without talking, we understood

As we walked through the park
We would talk about everything
This was our usual spot
On summer and winter days

Oh what a memory
Oh how beautiful that was
Sometimes I want to have that back
Should we reconnect or stay moved on?

## Goodbye My Past Love, Goodbye

I realized this morning that I never said goodbye
Now that I have real love, I must try
For once upon a time, you were in my past
Whatever was fate's reason, it did not last

You will always hold a special place in my heart
But right now, I'm working on a new romantic start
My current love right now, is something that's true
A new commitment is growing and I finally have let go of you

I realized that I didn't have full closure inside
That's because I chose to ignore it and I was full of pride
I realized that when you don't let your past go
Then eventually that past will start to show

And I feel that it's time for me to make progress
It's time for me to enjoy my current happiness
I did think about you today, but it was in a negative way
But I can't entertain it because that's cheating

Our paths in the past crossed more than one time
But you took it for granted and missed out on sunshine
And now that I have had a chance to move on
I am a better person today, I am really strong

You really had me wrapped around you
I said to myself, I will no longer be a fool
So now I must do what I need to do
And that is reach inside and let go of you

My love is growing with my new romance
I have to follow my heart and not blow this chance
Goodbye my past love, goodbye

## Is It a Mistake?

I think about you all the time
My heart still goes pitter pat
Although I try to move on
Our love I can't forget

I think about those memories
All the great times that we shared
I remember that feeling
Just knowing that you really cared

I can't deny our love
I can't deny what was true
Are these memories just an illusion?
Did I forget the abuse?

I thought about reconnecting
Would that decision be so wrong?
Will we repeat our same past?
Will we sing the same song?

I don't know what to do
I'm just confused
Will I really lose if I go back to you?

This decision is such a struggle
One that I don't want to make
No matter which path I go
One of those ways will be a huge mistake

## I Miss You

I miss those times
When we used to be together
I wish those times
Could have lasted forever

You kissed my mind
And filled my heart with laughter
You showed no sign
That our love would have left us

I miss the times that we spent
I wish those times would come again
I can't seem to get you out of my mind
Cause a love like you is so hard to find

I loved to see you smile
And I love the smell of your scent
You make me melt a thousand times
When I'm in your presence

You had my heart
In the palm of your hand
You've left your mark
Inside of my head

When I was with you
My gray sky turned blue
Now I'm missing you so bad
Can we start again and make us last?

## I'm Over The Anger

You think that I'm still mad at you
This is no longer the case
I've healed and I've moved on from you
I've accepted my mistakes

Sometimes love makes us take a turn
That we didn't see coming
I've lost and I've been burned
But now my strength is showing

I'm taking all the misery
That you brought into my life
I'm using it to be a better me
I'm not going lie down and cry

Too many tears were shed over you
Now I realize my life is better without you
You contacted me the other day
I have nothing left to say

I will not reopen that door
You're an ex for a reason
I'll be foolish to open up to hurting more
You were in my life for just a season

## I Must Move On

The words you speak
It means nothing to me
Because they're just words
There's no action

I'm at a point that I want us to end
I love you so much and it will heartbreaking
I can't continue living through this pain
I don't want my love to turn into hate

You've disrespected me for way too long
I let it got out of hand
I was too busy working every single day
I worked hard while you only played

You've become a burden
Even a blind man can see
You feel entitled
What makes you think you should be?

Love doesn't entitle you to treat me any kind of way
You've taken advantage of me being easy going
I don't like confrontation, I rather us speak what we have to say
All the yelling that you're doing, is not my kind of game

I'm getting to the point where I don't want to be here
I avoid coming home because I know an argument is near
I hate splitting up and I don't want this to end
But unfortunately I have to listen to my spirit

I know this is going to hurt both you and me
My heart will ache for an eternity
But I have to stop this cycle of what we're going through
My love, we must end, it's time for me to make that move

Don't Tell Me

When we first met there was a fire between us
And those images of our desire promised sweet love
I watched what happened as you changed on me
Who is this person you turned out to be?

I don't understand, I cared for you, I thought our love was true
I remember when I first met you, when we were new
From the start I gave you my heart
Why did you do this to me? You hurt me so deep

Don't tell me that you want me
When you lie to me so easily
Don't tell me that you'll be with me
When you plan to leave me lonely
Don't tell me that you love me
Don't say those words that you really don't mean, don't tell me
I'm not a fool I won't believe what you tell me

I will be strong through this pain
I will move on to another day
I won't stay down or settle for less
I know my worth, I deserve the best
I will find a love that's honest with me

I don't want to hear what you say
Don't tell me anything

## I'm Still in Love With You

You broke my heart on that February day
To my surprise, you turned and walked away
You left me in a state of mind that was displaced
There was no reason to treat me this way

I just can't stop dreaming of you everyday
You're in my mind, those thoughts won't dissipate
I cried for you until my heart poured out like rain
The reminiscence of you is driving me insane

How can you forget all those memories we shared?
I know inside that you still care
Let's keep our love alive and ignite a new romance
I'm thinking that we should give this another chance

Cause I'm still in love with you
I believe in my heart this is true
I feel you're still in love too
Let's get things back on track real soon

## This In-Between Game

One day I realized
What you mean to me
Though love is there inside
It don't seem to be
When I get close to you
You take a step back or two
And when I'm ready to move on
You show me that you don't want us done

I looked into your eyes
Trying to see what you see
I felt so blind
Because your heart don't match our scene
You're trying to make me feel like a fool
I'm not going to chase after you
Why do you wait until I'm leaving?
That's when you're ready to make a move

I looked into your eyes
They made me realize
That time's not on our side
You're letting love pass us by
I believed in you and me
I thought our love could be
But it was just a dream
It was just a fantasy

This in between game
Is so over played
My heart just can't take
Another disappointing ache

If we're going to be
Then let us be
But if we're not, then I'll set us free
I'm done with this in-between game

## Reconnecting to Your Energy

It's been a long time
Since I've heard your voice
You were on my mind
Reconnection was a possible choice

You contacted me out of the blue
It was sudden out of thin air
I don't know what to think of you
Do I want to take it there?

We decided to meet up
To see how our energies would sync
I thought I was over you
But now all these feelings are coming over me

I don't want to be stupid and rush into this
I don't want to repeat our past
I want to get to know you like a first date
Maybe we can take a different path

I'm open to reconnecting
As long as the bad things don't repeat
We both had some growing to do
Is this the right time for you and me?

Thank you for reading "Love Poems: Are You the One?" There were a lot of topics covered throughout this book. I hope this book has provided you with some insight and even help you discover some answers for your own personal situation. Love is such a broad topic. This book honed in on some situations that many people face on this road of love. Stay tuned for future books from Steve Ryan.

Steve Ryan is an accomplished singer/songwriter, actor and author. For more information on Steve Ryan, visit his website at www.SteveRyan.com .

www.ingramcontent.com/pod-product-compliance
Lightning Source LLC
Chambersburg PA
CBHW061252040426
42444CB00010B/2367